Affluent Patient Attraction for Cosmetic Surgeons

Affluent Patient Attraction for Cosmetic Surgeons

5 Magnetic Ways To Transform Your Medical Practice
By Attracting Patients Who Pay More.

by

Chris Sewell

www.ChrisSewellDigitalMedia.nyc

DISCLAIMER

The author has made every attempt to be as accurate and complete as possible in the creation of this publication/PDF, however he / she does not warrant or represent at any time that the contents within are accurate due to the rapidly changing nature of the Internet. The author assumes no responsibility for errors, omissions, or contrary interpretation of the subject matter herein. Any perceived slights of specific persons, peoples, or organizations other published materials are unintentional and used solely for educational purposes only.

This information is not intended for use as a source of legal, business, accounting or financial advice. All readers are advised **to seek services of competent professionals in legal, business, accounting, and finance field.** No representation is made or implied that the reader will do as well from using the suggested techniques, strategies, methods, systems, or ideas; rather it is presented for news value only.

The author does not assume any responsibility or liability **whatsoever** for what you choose to do with this information. Use your own judgment. Consult appropriate professionals before starting a business. Any perceived remark, comment or use of organizations, people mentioned and any resemblance to characters living, dead or otherwise, real or fictitious does not mean that they support this content in any way.

There are no guarantees of income made, traffic delivered or other promises of any kind. Readers are cautioned to reply on their own judgment about their individual circumstances to act accordingly. By reading any document, the reader agrees that under no circumstances is the author responsible for any losses, direct or indirect, that are incurred as a result of use of the information contained within this document, including - but not limited to errors, omissions, or inaccuracies.

Table of Contents

HOW TO USE THIS REPORT TO *TRANSFORM* YOUR MEDICAL PRACTICE IN THIS

New Economy

Competition is forcing you to lower your prices...and that stinks! You're not charging patients as much as you're worth, *which isn't fair to you.*

Thanks to the Internet, **the New Economy gives potential patients more power now than ever before**. Prices for what you charge are very transparent. This forces you to lower your fees...to work more hours ...and to spend less time with family.

For example...

- In 2011, the average price for Botox treatment was $365. Today, sites like Groupon and Living Social offer deals for as low as $99.

- You may have charged $1,600 for liposuction in 1992, and then $2,860 in 2011. Flash forward to today and patients can find these services for $999.

- The cost of laser skin resurfacing was about $1,200 in 2011. Today, there are coupon sites offering laser resurfacing for a mere $299

FIERCE COMPETITION HITS YOU FROM MANY ANGLES

In this New Economy, it's not just the older man with a much younger woman. According to AARP, at least one in three women between ages 40 and 70 dates a younger man.

This has fueled a large demand for anti-aging and weight loss services among men and women. As more people demand cosmetic procedures to look younger, more physicians began providing them.

There are very few barriers for professionals to enter this lucrative field.

In recent years there has been a proliferation of medical spas opening their doors nationwide. Everyone from entrepreneurs to physicians is seeking to take advantage of this new segment of the spa and retail healthcare industries.

DENTISTS, GYNECOLOGISTS, BARELY TRAINED SPA TECHNICIANS – IT SEEMS LIKE EVERYONE'S OFFERING ANTI-AGING TREATMENTS THESE DAYS

Dentists giving a little Botox in between filling cavities or gynecologists giving Botox between Pap smears -- tend to opt for quicker training in cosmetic procedures. **The International Society of Cosmetogynecology** offers weekend workshops that promote plastic surgery as an extension of gynecology.

With social media sites handing out cosmetic-treatment discounts like candy, it's easy for your potential patients to get caught up in bargain-hunting ...regardless of the possible negative side effects. Competition is great when you're a buyer, because you get lower prices for goods and services. When you're a seller, competition hurts your earning potential.

As a medical professional in the anti-aging and weight loss field, you have many competitors nibbling away at the *higher prices you could charge*. Forcing you to work longer hours, charge lower fees, and earn less.

You know your services are worth more than you're currently charging -- but, how can you charge more and not lose patients? Keep reading and I'll reveal how you can *charge more than your competition*, earn more each year, and spend less time in the office.

COUPON SITES LIKE GROUPON AND LIVING SOCIAL ARE STEALING YOUR PATIENTS

If you check out coupon sites like **Groupon** and **Living Social**, you'll find numerous medical-related services at deep discounts.

- Botox, laser hair removal, laser facial resurfacing...*at deep discounts*

- Spider vein and brown spot removal...*at deep discounts*

How can you compete? Each year you lower prices to keep your income stable, while working longer hours. Does this make you angry? **It should.**

The Internet gives medical professionals, like you, a ton of competition. The New Economy also means it's more important to differentiate yourself from your competitors.

As a result of the 2007 Great Recession, many businesses that catered to the *"general-masses"* got smart. They added a **high-end component** to their business model to make themselves **recession-proof.**

REBRAND YOUR BUSINESS TO STAY AHEAD OF YOUR COMPETITION

Take for example, **Hallmark Gold Crown**. You've no doubt purchased greeting cards from this well known store chain. In 2004, Hallmark operated 4,000 stores, targeting the "general masses" who are typically bargain hunters.

Hallmark *rebranded itself* as HMK to provide gifts and cards to affluent customers. Their new stores have a more luxurious look and feel than their old Hallmark Gold Crown stores.

> I know this is only one example. I don't want to load this book up with a million more examples. You might get bored.

Companies that completely rely on the "general-masses" to grow their business, will be forever controlled by the ups and downs of the economy. This is because, the "general-masses" are controlled by the ups and downs of the economy. Hallmark is transforming its business. **You should transform yours too.**

Many jobs that employed the "general-masses" will never return. Even more jobs will vanish in the future. If your medical practice is focused on attracting the "average" worker, you'll find that they are very price-sensitive.

This is why you want to transform your business to <u>attract affluent patients</u> who are highly skilled workers or business owners -- where price isn't their main concern.

CHANGE YOUR PATIENTS FROM THE "MASSES" TO THE "AFFLUENT"

Coupon sites like Groupon and Living Social offer deep discounts on anti-aging and weight loss services. How can you possibly compete with that if you service the same type of clients as these discount sites?

Don't try to compete. You won't win. **Move your business to a new model** and you'll win those affluent patients.

Transform your business into a model that caters to patients who rarely look for the lowest fee provider. You want patients who are more concerned with the unique experience, and knowledge that you offer...

...but, more importantly, you want patients who'll pay you a premium for <u>**your ability to clear the confusion in their heads about what services are best for them**</u>.

If you want to join the ranks of the *'Super-Elite, Recession-Proof'* medical professionals -- you must go where the money is and ___plant your flag now___. There are far too many physicians who want to cater to the general-masses and compete with coupon sites that offer very low fees.

You shouldn't be one of them.

If you already have affluent patients, it's time you got more of them. I must admit, the work to attract affluent patients is greater than what's required to attract the "general masses".

Prospecting the "general-masses" is low-hanging fruit.

I FELL VICTIM TO THAT SAME THINKING DURING THE EARLY YEARS OF MY LEAD-GENERATING, MARKETING CONSULTING PRACTICE.

Back in 2000, I focused on the small business owner and the part-time business owner who wanted to grow.

It took me about 5 years before I realized I was doing it all wrong.

When I started implementing affluent client attraction secrets revealed by **Dan Kennedy, Pam Danziger, William Danko, and Mark Penn,** I realized there was a niche to every niche.

Every niche has 90% who don't have much money and 10% with a bunch of money. Every niche has this dynamic. I challenge you to name any niche that doesn't. When you market your practice to affluent patients -- your business will have less competition because your competitors will target patients on the lower economic end of the ladder.

YOU MUST UNDERSTAND WHO THESE AFFLUENT PATIENTS ARE

Your approach to <u>attracting affluent patients</u> must be **very different** than your approach to attracting the "general-masses" as patients. The affluent hangout in different places...they read different publications...they have different fears...their concerns are more complex. I'll point you in the right direction to hook them and reel them in one fish at a time.

The extra work you must put into transforming your business to attract the affluent is not bigger than the opportunity in front of you. It's not 10x more difficult to attract a high-paying patient than a discount seeking patient.

...you just have to understand how to do it.

You must be a little smarter...a little more systematic...and a little more targeted in your approach.

I'll show you how to do all of this in this report. You just need to put my techniques into action. Targeting the **right** affluent patient-prospects will be critical to your success. I will discuss this in detail.

THE MEDIA HAS YOU THINKING THAT... AFFLUENT PATIENTS ARE HARD TO FIND ...IGNORE THAT STUFF

If you listen to the media -- whenever there's a market downturn, you would think everyone is pinching pennies and cutting up their credit cards.

If you focus on the news -- you might think that affluent people are hurting financially. You might also believe your practice is doomed to take a downturn whenever the economy falters, because all of your clients are taking a financial hit.

If your practice caters to clients with networths under $500K, you would be correct. Your practice will suffer when the economy craters.

Running a business that caters to people who have a networth under $500K means you own a business that is controlled by the economy.

ALL IS NOT LOST...
YOU CAN REINVENT YOUR PRACTICE...
AND IF YOU KEEP READING, I'LL SHOW YOU HOW

Despite the challenges you face in this industry, some Medical Professionals have transformed their businesses by attracting more affluent patients than they can handle. These Medical Professionals are enjoying more free time, while earning more yearly income.

No matter where your practice is located. No matter what condition it's in. **You can attract more affluent patients than you can handle.**

This "special class" of patients wants to pay you higher fees, even if you charge more than your competitors. Just follow the little-known, but effective techniques I'll reveal to you in this guide.

New Opportunity

TO FINALLY DISTANCE YOURSELF FROM YOUR COMPETITION...AND *REBRAND* YOUR PRACTICE

According to Spectrem Group Research, the fastest growing demographic is the "mass-affluent", households with a networth of $500K to $1MM.

These people are the "special class" of patients you should start targeting today. Listening to the media -- you would think everyone price shops...looks for coupons online, and haggles to get lower prices.

That simply isn't the case.

Demand For Your Medical Services ....Has DOUBLED

According to the American Society for Aesthetic Plastic Surgery (ASAPS), 10 years ago, 13.1 million anti-aging procedures were performed.

Today, it's 25.3 million.

Yes, there are millions of people who want to turn back the age clock and spice up their love lives.

It's estimated that 10 years from today, 55 million anti-aging procedures will be performed in the United States...that's an annual growth of 8% a year.

Minimally-invasive cosmetic services are growing at 28% each year.

DESPITE THE INCREASED DEMAND FOR WHAT YOU DO, YOUR FEES ARE FLAT - - BECAUSE YOU'RE TARGETING THE WRONG TYPE OF PATIENT

If your marketing is targeted towards anyone who wants your medical services --- you're making a big mistake. You need to start targeting a special class of patient. I'm talking about the "mass-affluent".

Who are the "mass-affluent"?

They're the people that moved out of the "middle-class" to a place a few economic steps upwards. The media likes to talk about the "disappearing" middle class. As if some space ship sucked them off the earth.

Here's what happened to the old middle class...

One-third moved down the economic ladder because their skills became obsolete.

The factory worker, the assembly line manager, the guy who worked with his hands to feed his family -- replaced by either automation or the Chinese factory that produces quicker results at a lower price. The other two-thirds of the old middle-class moved up the economic ladder.

They embraced the Internet and started online businesses. They used the Internet to research how to start a business or improve their traditional business. They learned to outsource certain tasks to be competitive with larger companies.

These two-thirds are what's called the **"mass-affluent."** These are the types of patients you should target, because they're far less likely to shop for discounts when buying anti-aging procedures.

They might want a toothbrush at a discount...but when it comes to a tummy-tuck, botox, laser facial resurfacing, or other anti-aging procedures -- they want to be treated like celebrities.

And, they're willing to pay you that celebrity price.

The second group that you should target is the **"affluent"**. They have a networth of $1MM to $3MM, according to Wealth Engine. These two groups of affluent patients can truly transform your medical practice

WHO ARE THESE PATIENTS WILLING TO PAY YOU HIGHER FEES?

Many of the "mass-affluent" work high-paying jobs because they have specialized skills. They're middle to upper level managers at tech firms and staffing agencies, who used their high wages to buy real estate to grow their networth

If you want more free time outside the office and you also want to earn more income -- **fill your pipeline with affluent patients.**

The good news for you is there are **13.5MM households** with a networth between $500K and $1MM, according to *US Census* data. Many live in your state, or are willing to drive across state lines to reach you -- if you truly differentiate yourself from a local competitor.

This class of affluent looks pretty normal.

They look and talk just like you and most shop where you shop each day. Read the *'Millionaire Next Door'*, by William Danko if you want an in-depth education on their norms.

Let me give you more facts about the mass-affluent discussed in *U.S. Federal Reserve* studies, the *'Millionaire Next Door'*, and *US Census Data*.

The Mass-Affluent

This demographical pool is the fastest growing in the world right now.

As more people embrace the Internet to learn how to create wealth and deepen their education on a wide variety of topics -- there'll be more mass-affluent patients for your medical practice than you can handle.

Here's what you need to know about them.

- They have a networth from $500,000 to $1MM.

- There are 21.6 million such households according to **Pam Danziger** of **Unity Marketing**. (US Census data claims 13.5MM households)

- Most of their networth is tied up in retirement accounts.

- They read publications by **Suze Orman** and **Money** magazine to learn how to make smart decisions with their money.

- 60% of the women in these two-person households are involved in all investment decisions. *(Don't make the mistake of thinking that the men make all money decisions.)*

- They are typically a two-person salaried household that earns $100,000 to $250,000 yearly

- They used to be in the traditional middle-class group, but they've upgraded their skills

- They include the small business owners that learned how to start or grow their business from resources found online. (This also includes blue- and white- collar workers with specialized skills.)

- They shop at Saks, Bloomingdales, and Nordstroms to splurge a little, but also loves to shop at Target and Wal-Mart .

- This group aspires to be affluent, but values staying within their budget

- They are highly educated. They attended major universities and received advanced degrees.

The Affluent

Then you have the affluent patient-prospect. These are people with a networth of $1MM to $3MM. This group has the largest discretionary income than any generation before them. This new breed of affluent is spending their wealth, especially on anti-aging and weight loss services.

- They have a networth from $1MM to $MM. Age 35-55.

- There are 7.5 million such households according to *Pam Danziger* of *Unity Marketing*

- Over the last 2 decades, this group has exploded with new households.

- The flattening of the globe has spawned more of these millionaires all over the world.

- Many live in middle-class neighborhoods. Some live next door to you. The "shadow" millionaire according to *William Danko* in *'The Millionaire Next Door'*.

- They shop at Saks, Bloomingdales, and Nordstroms to splurge, but also not ashamed to shop at Target and Wal-Mart to blend into the middle-class scene.

- They read The Wall Street Journal and Forbes

- They may own a second, small home outside their primary state.

- Follows political and world events, and lean Conservative.

SUPER SWEET SPOT FOR HIGH-PAYING PATIENTS
WHO WILL RETURN MULTIPLE TIMES

If you really want to focus like a laser beam on the best patients to totally transform your medical practice -- focus on two classes of people: **Women Over 40 and Men Over 50.**

These two groups will fill your pipeline with more "high-paying" patients than you can handle.

I'll go more in-depth on the best ways to approach these two groups later in this guide. There are more than enough affluent patient-prospects to help you build a recession-proof practice.

When I started targeting affluent clients for my lead-generation, marketing consulting practice -- I enjoyed more income with fewer clients and less stress.

It also allowed me to better focus on my clients...connect with them more emotionally...and get referrals without asking for them. That's what attracting affluent clients (or patients) can do for one's business.

WHY YOU SHOULD REINVENT YOUR PRACTICE
BY ATTRACTING "MASS-AFFLUENT" & AFFLUENT PATIENTS

You'll Enjoy Less Competition

Your competitors don't know what you're about to know. You now have the unfair advantage.

Your competitors think the affluent are a small group that's hard to reach. After you complete this report, you'll discover how to get them excited about you and comfortable enough to hire you.

Most Medical Professionals spend money and time to attract the 90% of the population with less than $500K in networth. These professionals are intimidated to market to affluent patient-prospects. **Don't be one of them**

It's crowded at the bottom and competition is fierce for patients looking for coupons, discounts and specials. You'll find less medical professionals targeting affluent patients.

Shocking news: Not everyone price shops. You don't need to discount your fees to get patients. Just target a DIFFERENT type of patient. I'll show you how.

The affluent have less people trying to sell services to them. This is why you need to target them more -- but you need the right type of system that I'll reveal to you very soon.

They're Less Price Sensitive

According to a 2012 Nielsen Report, only 10% of people buy based on price. This is the same 10% most medical professionals target...maybe even you.

I was part of this 10% crowd growing up in Brooklyn, NY. We were on food stamps for about 8-months. My mother only purchased food on sale, and if she had a coupon for it.

There's another 20% who never buy based on price. It's not part of their buying criteria. Price isn't in their DNA. The affluent are more concerned with the **experience they get working with you.** They're not interested in searching for lower fees.

If you help them _clear confusion in their heads_ about which procedures are best for them, **they'll pay you more than what you get paid now.** I'm going to discuss clearing the confusion for patients later. This is how you differentiate yourself from your competitors. This allows you to charge higher fees, while working with fewer patients.

You can't simply offer a cookie cutter type service to the affluent. They'll go somewhere else that offers a customized approach. In my lead-generating, marketing consulting practice to medical professionals -- I offer a customized approach to help my clients attract more affluent patients who are willing to pay higher fees.

You must do the same if you want to attract more affluent patients.

They're Loyal Patients

...if you don't ignore them

Do you like being ignored?

No one likes being ignored.

The affluent are more likely to get repeat services from you, just as long as, you don't screw things up and ignore them once you get them.

When you offer anti-aging or weight loss procedures, you should outline a list of services to offer patients based on the last service performed.

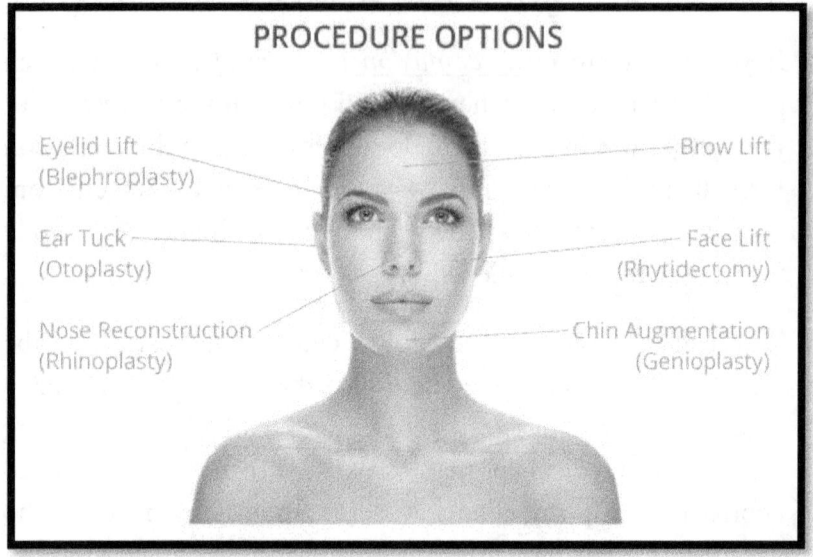

PROCEDURE OPTIONS

Eyelid Lift
(Blephroplasty)

Ear Tuck
(Otoplasty)

Nose Reconstruction
(Rhinoplasty)

Brow Lift

Face Lift
(Rhytidectomy)

Chin Augmentation
(Genioplasty)

<u>*Let's take the face for example...*</u>

If a patient gets a Rhinoplasty or a laser facial resurface, after they heal, you should offer them maybe an eyelid lift...ear tuck...brow lift...or Genioplasty.

Don't wait for them to contact you about what service they should get next. Take a proactive approach and tell them what they should get next.

Patients who price shop *(the general masses of people),* will use whatever service offers them the biggest coupon discount. It's time for you to reinvent your business and target affluent people who are concerned with quality, not price.

Ritz Carlton customers *(affluent)* are more loyal than Holiday Inn customers *(general masses).* A Holiday Inn customer is looking for the cheapest room to lay his head. Red Roof, Quality Inn, Best Western -- it doesn't matter to him as long as he gets the lowest price.

> Monthly newsletters *(snail mail, not email)*...makes it becomes easy to stay in contact with patients (or prospects) about what you can do for them.

When you deal with Ritz Carlton type patients, they will not accept being ignored. They expect a newsletter, video seminar, or special event to hold their attention. This allows you to get more of their money.

They're a Better Source Of Referrals

Birds of a feather, flock together. Millionaires tend to surround themselves with other millionaires. Men and women, who are comfortable getting age reversal procedures, hang around other men and women who feel the same way.

When your affluent patients tell their millionaire friends that you helped them look and feel 10 years younger -- **it's easy to get referrals.**

> **The real reasons why people want to look & feel younger:**
>
> • Find a new partner
>
> • Better sex more often
>
> • Look great naked

If you do a great job with them, their affluent friends will know. If you make a mess of things and ignore them, they'll know about that too and ***avoid you like you had a the plague.***

Imagine what your medical practice would look like if you were to take advantage of the opportunity in front of you today. Imagine putting a system in place that attracts affluent patients to your practice like a magnet.

You could work less hours, manage fewer patients, and spend more fun time with family. You can do all of this while making more money.

That's exactly what happened to *Dr. Giri Singh, Surgeon at Rosedale Ivy Surgery*. He implemented the 5 New Economy techniques that I teach in this resource to transform his medical practice and attract affluent patients.

Another medical professional who is working less and making more is *Dr. Dan Sinhoff, of the Sinhoff Medical Spa & Weight Loss clinic.* Dan repositioned his practice targeting men over 50 and women over 40, with a networth of at least $500K.

According to AARP, someone turns 50, every 7.5 seconds. Every day, more than 11,500 Americans hit the big Five O. This is a huge opportunity for you to transform your business.

The **American Society of Plastic Surgeons** reported that total cosmetic procedures for men rose 22% from 2000 through 2012. These guys are trying to keep up with their younger girlfriends, look younger on the job, or improve their chances of getting a new job.

What would your medical practice look like if you acquired more affluent patients who want to pay you twice what you currently charge? **Now, imagine that happening within the next 12 months.**

Here are five ways you can start doing it immediately...

Reinvent Your Business

With These 5 New Economy Ways To Attract Affluent Patients Who Will Pay You More

New Economy Rule #1:
Develop your personal story — Your big "WHY"

This is your deep, personal, sometimes uncomfortable story of why you've dedicated your life to the medical profession.

When I say a <u>deep personal</u> *"WHY"*, I mean you must convey to prospects the most emotional things in your life that pushed you into being a medical professional.

Don't try to play it safe and give a story that makes you comfortable.

Your big *"WHY"* can't be something you feel totally comfortable telling a stranger on the street, such as, <u>*"I value health because I've always been a healthy responsible person."*</u>

That's a very positive, unemotional, and safe reason. This is bad!

> When I was 14 and found those food stamps on my mom's kitchen table, I was ashamed that we were so poor. I thought food stamps were for those poor kids who lived in Albany housing project 4 blocks down the street from my Brooklyn home.
>
> That's the day I realized that I was just as poor and I needed to find away above it.
>
> This is why I'm in business for myself. To control how much money I earn so I never need to accept a government hand-out.

You need to connect emotionally with your prospect. Losing weight and anti-aging are emotional. If you want affluent people to trust you with cutting, reshaping, or taking stuff out of their bodies. **You need to first connect with them emotionally.**

If you said...

"My parents divorced when I was 10. My father all but admitted he found a younger and sexier women he would rather be with. He just wasn't physically attracted to my mom anymore. I became a medical professional to help men and women save their marriages from boredom. It's amazing how a more youthful looking face and body can inject new excitement into a marriage or give someone the confidence to start a new one."

That's a good, big reason *"why"*. It's emotional.

I just made that story up, but can you see how that story would connect with someone emotionally?

Your personal story might contain elements that resonate with your potential patient. Maybe your potential patient is recently divorced and needs the confidence to find someone new.

> Your personal story is used in the remaining 4 techniques for attracting affluent patients. So take it seriously.
>
> If you play it safe and create an unemotional story, you'll find it very difficult to attract and maintain affluent patients.

Your story must have uncomfortable elements to it to connect with people emotionally. Even if your prospect doesn't connect with your personal story -- the fact that you opened up emotionally helps your prospect trust you because you trusted them enough tell your story.

Your best patients are men over 50 and women over 40 -- divorced in the last 6-months, who want to start a new life with a new body and new hope for the future.

They need you to help them realize this new future. I'm going to talk more about these two groups to help you find them. I'm spending a lot of time on developing your big *"WHY"* because a poorly crafted one will cripple your success with the affluent.

- Who influenced your beliefs about health and life?

- What moment of truth shaped your philosophy about anti-aging and weight loss?

First, the affluent want an emotional connection with you. This creates trust instantly. Then, they want to know about your technical qualifications.

- Why are you so passionate about serving your patients?

- Why are you the best person to understand their family and life concerns?

- What makes you more than just another "doctor"?

Most elite medical professionals have powerful personal stories. They have a biography that reflects, in an intimate way, the emotional and social circumstances of their career choice and the unique motivations that promoted a career in the medical field.

New Economy Rule #2:
Target Men Over 50 & Women Over 40 Years Old

This is the sweet spot for finding patients who want your medical services and can pay high fees to get them.

Mark Penn wrote a book entitled, "**Microtrends**". In this book he details the rise of the 'Cougars', affluent women over 40 who want to date younger men. He also makes mention of Men over 50 who want to date younger women.

In his book, Mr. Penn notes, *"...the natural instinct for people with success to trade that success for sexual attractiveness. And, what was once achievable only by older men with money is now within reach of women with power and accomplishment (and money)."*

If you know many affluent people, you'll notice a natural instinct for them to leverage their success and money into youth, sex, longevity, even immortality.

You should start exploiting these facts and target your marketing towards this demographic. It's not enough to just send a brochure in the mail. That's not how you do it.

In the **"Direct Mail"** section of this guide, I'll show you the smart way to use direct mail to attract affluent patients.

> Men are catching up to women when it comes to a willingness towards spend money to buy youth and attractiveness. This usually occurs when they turn 50.

According to a study by the *Aesthetic Surgery Journal*, 81% of breast enhancement patients and 68% of other body enhancement patients, reported improvements in sexual satisfaction.

More than half of these patients said they were able to orgasm more easily after their surgery. Smart medical professionals are using this information in their marketing when targeting **women over 40 and men over 50.**

You should too, because this demographic responds very well to the youth equals better sex comparison.

New Economy Rule #3:
Clear The Confusion Going On
In The Heads Of Potential Patients

Your patient-prospects are aging and confused.

With thousands of anti-aging products and dozens of weight loss procedures flooding the market -- these men and women need someone to clear the confusion in their heads.

If you can clear that confusion, you have an excellent chance to get their business.

According to the *American Academy of Dermatology* in Schaumburg, Illinois -- **94% of women are confused by their anti-aging options.** Cosmetic surgeons are competing with each other. Medical spas, wellness centers, and weight loss clinics are also competing with others in their industry.

...and, all are competing against each other for consumer dollars.

Consumers have a dizzying array of medical professionals who can provide anti-aging and weight loss solutions.

In this New Economy, *you must distinguish yourself* from providers in your industry and those outside your industry. If you don't, you'll end up competing on price -- and competing on price is not how you grow profits. Competing on price puts your medical practice in a race to the bottom.

You end up working more hours, for less money. Those hours at the office take away precious time you could spend with family and friends. Ultimately, this causes you to resent what you do.

Potential patients want you to first educate than about the positives and negatives of various anti-aging and weight loss solutions. Consumers will pay more money to the medical professional who takes the time to educate them first.

You don't want to do this one-on-one. That takes too much time. You need to leverage your time. There are media you can use to help prospects clear the confusion in their heads about the advantages and disadvantages of the various services you offer.

- Offer a PDF special report as a download from your website

- Hold an online video seminar: Goto Meeting or Google hangout *(a favorite of my clients)*

- Mail a DVD of a pre-recorded online seminar to people who request it.

- Post a pre-recorded video on your website answering various questions.

You need to start leveraging different forms of media to help prospects clear the confusion in their heads regarding which procedures are best for them.

New Economy Rule #4:
Use Direct Mail In A Smart Way

The wrong way to use direct mail is to send a brochure to a list of people. If you've done that before, you know it's a failed strategy.

How to be smart about direct mail...

I know you may have a sour taste in your mouth regarding direct mail. Some list broker most likely convinced you to *mail 10,000 expensive brochures* to a list he sold you.

But, the mailing flopped big time.

The problem <u>isn't</u> that direct mail stinks. Direct mail works great **if** you get three stars in alignment:

- The right message

- The right prospects

- The right delivery method

The **right message** isn't how many years you've been in business or that you received your medical degree from an Ivy League school.

The right message is:

- Look Great Naked In The Next 6 Weeks

- New Face, New Body...New Man...New Perfect Life

- Confused About Which Anti-Aging Procedure Is Best For You?

- Get A Better Orgasm...Knock 10 Years Off Your Face & Body!

The **right prospects** are not anyone from 18-68 who will pay you. The sweet spot are recently divorced women over 40 and men over 50. Let's add a few more qualifications to help you get a more targeted list.

- Has a gym membership at an expensive club (this means they're already spending money to improve themselves)

- Has purchased expensive beauty products (They value attraction)

- Networth over $500K

Your list will not be large. It might be a few hundred or less than 5,000. The list will be super targeted. The **right delivery** method isn't a brochure stuffed inside of a #10 size envelope. Do what I do for my medical professional clients.

Create a kit called...

> *"Clear The Confusion: 5 Things You Need*
> *To Know About Anti-Aging Procedures That Most*
> *Professionals Are Too Afraid Tell You!"*

This kit should include a...

- Report

- DVD

- Testimonials

- Newsletter

- Certificate to an event or consultation session.

The **report and DVD** answers questions about surgery versus minimally-invasive options for looking years younger or losing weight.

The **Testimonial sheet** or booklet contains words from your satisfied patients. A video testimonial DVD is more powerful.

The **newsletter** demonstrates your knowledge in the anti-aging and weight-loss fields.

Finally, the **certificate** offers the prospect an opportunity to consult with you to better understand their options. Holding an event or seminar where you answer questions is even more powerful.

New Economy Rule #5:
The BIGGEST SECRET Of ALL
– You Need A Sophisticated "Follow-up" System

You can do everything else correctly --

... *develop your big "why"*

... *target women over 40 and men over 50 who are recently divorced*

... *clear the confusion in their heads by educating them*

... *use smart direct mail strategies to reach the best patient prospects*

But, if your follow up system is primitive *(like the one on the next page)*, your results will be poor.

A primitive follow up system...

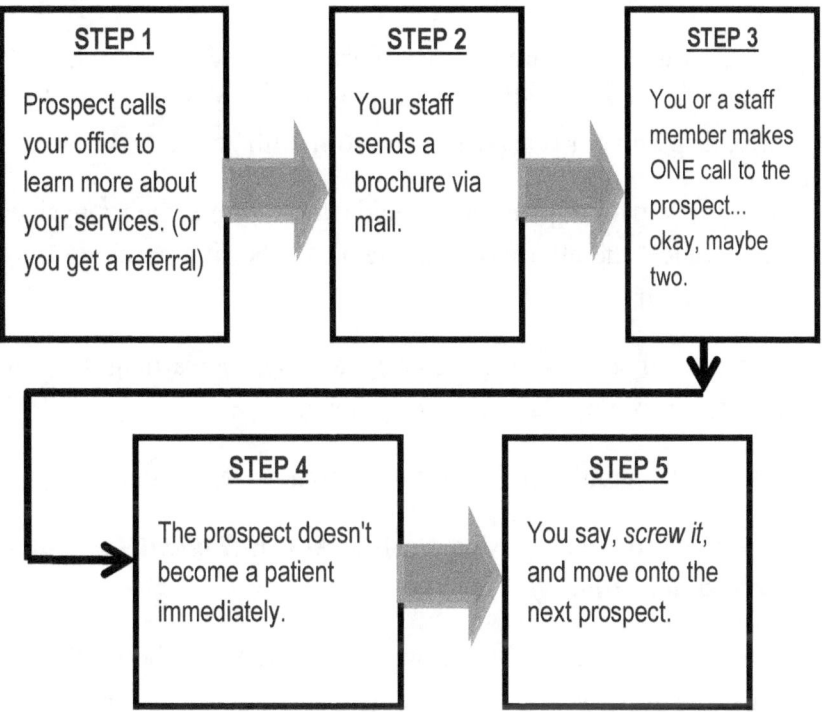

If your follow up system looks something like what's described above, you'll have a very difficult time attracting more affluent patients than you can handle. Affluent people expect you to work harder to get them as patients.

All medical professionals showed at least once or twice with a brochure and a call.

YOU NEED A SOPHISTICATED FOLLOW-UP SYSTEM LIKE THIS...

If you want to separate yourself from your competitors, your follow up system will need some steroids. You need to drip, drip, drip on your prospects over a 6-month period.

Very few patient-prospects decide to improve their physical appearance one afternoon, and then call the first brochure they get in the mail.

The idea of some stranger cutting, slicing, or rearranging their body parts requires some serious thought.

...like 6-12 months of thinking and mental preparation.

You need to develop what I call a P.I.C.F *(Patient Incubator Conversion Funnel)*.

This funnel should use various media types to show affluent prospects that you're competent, in demand by others, and caring.

The affluent don't easily hand over their bodies to just anyone. However, once you get them as a patient -- as long as you don't ignore them -- they will come back to you for many more procedures.

What you need is a sophisticated follow up system that most of your competitors are too lazy to implement. Their laziness can be your victory.

Your follow-up system should look something like this...

A SOPHISTICATED FOLLOW-UP SYSTEM
THAT ATTRACTS AFFLUENT PATIENTS

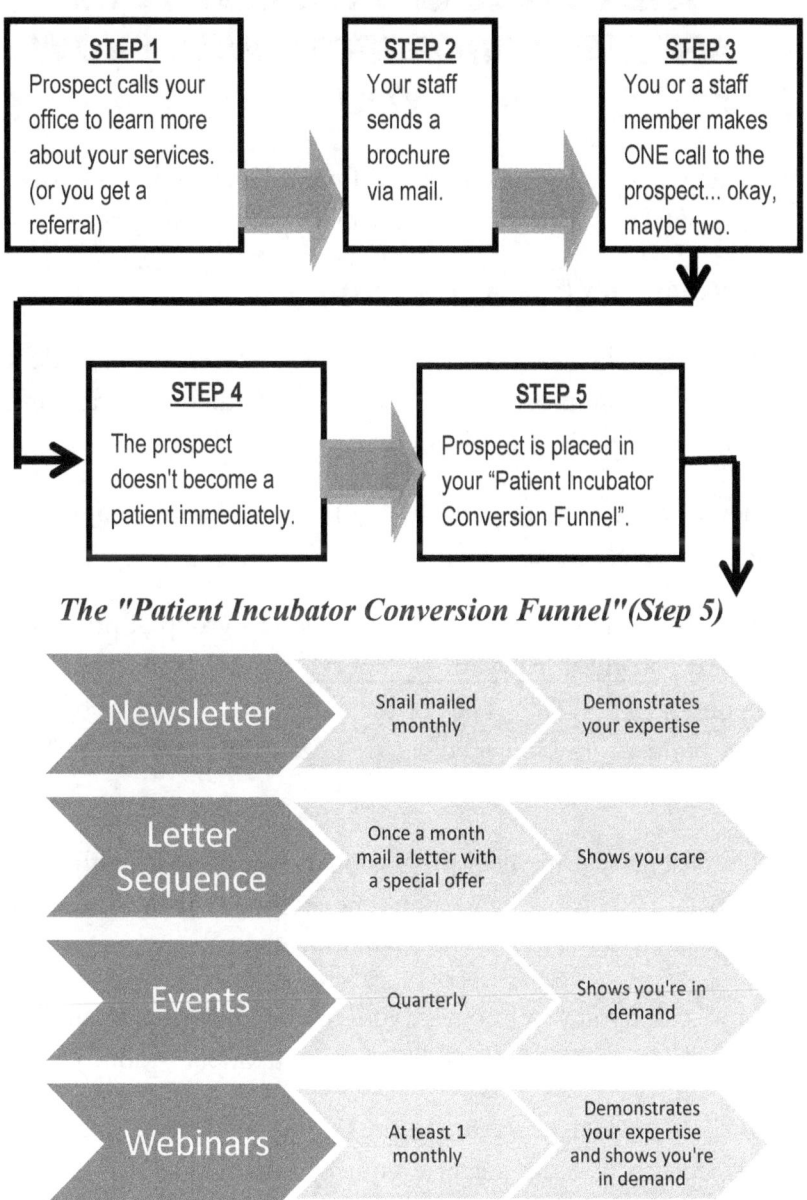

The *"Patient Incubator Conversion Funnel"(Step 5)*

Your prospects need to soften in your incubator for 6-12 months before you give up on them. I can assure you that most of your competition isn't doing this.

THE LEVELS OF INTEREST YOUR AFFLUENT PROSPECTS WILL SHOW YOU

Affluent patient prospects have different levels of interest when they contact you for more details about your medical services.

1. Ready Now (5% of prospects)

Every physician dreams of finding the **"Ready Now"** patient-prospect. These prospects have already decided they want anti-aging or weight loss services.

They've done their research. They know which procedures are best for themselves.

The **"Ready Now"** prospect is the smallest group of prospects. Usually, **around 5% of prospects** are ready to make an appointment "NOW". They're the easiest to convert -- but you can't build a growing medical practice catering only to those who are "ready now".

The reason most medical professionals like the **"Ready Now"** prospect is because you don't need much of a systematic follow-up process to convert them to patients.

They call...you call back...you make initial consultation appointment... they agree to be your next patient -- done deal.

You'll have lots of competition relying on converting these prospects to patients because your competition will follow-up at least once. If your competitor gets to the prospect before you, then you lose.

Top medical professionals don't expect to build their practices on the hopes of meeting the "**Ready Now**" patient-prospect. Only ordinary medical professionals depend on this class of prospect.

2. Very Interested (5% of prospects)

The **"Very Interested"** prospect is the next best prospect to find.

They require a bit more follow-up. If your follow-up system includes more than just one call or mailed brochure -- you have a good chance of converting the **"Very Interested"** prospect to a patient.

Unfortunately, this group is only about 5% of the prospects you'll find.

3. Low Interest (85% of prospects)

This is the **largest group of prospects** you'll encounter and this is where all the money sits and waits.

This represents a huge opportunity for you to transform your practice. But, you'll need a very robust, systematic follow-up process like my *"Patient Incubator Conversion Funnel"*.

A robust follow-up system lasts for about 6-months and includes about 30 contacts using email, print, audio, and video formats.

This relentless follow-up pushes the "**Low Interest**" prospect into the "**Very Interested**" group, and then eventually into a "**Ready Now**" prospect.

4. Doesn't Really Care At All (5% of prospects)

If you target your prospects correctly, this group should never be an issue.

Where you advertise, where you network, where you write articles and conduct webinars --

...determines if you'll attract prospects interested in anti-aging and weight loss services.

In this group you'll usually find your competitors and tire kickers responding to your marketing. These people are just curious about what you're up to.

Putting It All Together

What do you think your business would look like if you incorporated all the strategies I discussed with you in this guide?

Do you want to find out?

For existing clients that qualify, we can put this entire system together for your practice.

Here's how...

Apply To Join Our Client-Family

GROW YOUR INCOME IN THE NEXT 12-MONTHS
MORE THAN YOU HAVE OVER THE LAST 12-YEARS

As I told you earlier -- In this New Economy, you don't want just any type of patient. You want more "dream" patients...*(more affluent patients)*...to make your business recession-proof.

A few new slots have opened in my digital marketing consulting practice for successfully cosmetic surgeons who want to double (or triple) their practice in The next 12-months

Unfortunately for them *(but fortunate for you)*... I had to let a few clients go who were not as motivated to transform their practices as I initially thought.

I'm looking for a few "dream" medical professional clients to fill these slots so that I can bring the owners massive windfalls... and **more free time outside the office.**

If you're that client, **I'll personally work with you one-on-one** in your medical practice to help you...

- get more affluent patients who will pay you higher fees

- double or triple your revenue in the next 12 months

- make your competition irrelevant in the minds of your prospects

You Pay Nothing Out Of Pocket, Ever

Here's why...

The first thing I'm going to do is personally help you create a strategic plan to attract more high-paying patients.

There's no charge for this and it only takes about 30-45 minutes for us to do together. Yes, we must work together on the initial plan... *(After doing this type of thing since 2010, I've gotten pretty good at fast results).*

I'll even do most of the heavy lifting for you. I'll tell you exactly what to send, how to position your offer...and how to bring in back-end profits from additional services.

At the end of this initial planning session, one of these three things will happen:

1. **You'll love the plan and decide to implement it on your own.** If this is the case, I'll wish you the best of

luck and ask that you keep in touch with me to let me know how you're doing.

2. **You'll love the plan and ask to become my client** so I can personally help you execute, maximize, and profit from it ASAP.

3. If that's the case, we'll knock it out of the park ...**And that's a promise.** Every single one of my clients gets results. Literally. Every. Single. One.

It's really that simple and there's no catch.

Think about this.

The "worst" that can happen is you waste 30-45 minutes of your time. The best that can happen is **we work together one-on-one** to generate new affluent patients for your practice. It's time *affluent patients* start considering you! I want to develop a plan to make that a reality.

Transform Your Medical Practice
...for FREE!

Here's how it works...

First, we get on the phone, one on one, and go over your practice. I take a look at what you've got, what you're doing *(and not doing),* and what you want to achieve in the next 12-months.

Once we have those "raw materials", I help you come up with a strategic plan of action to **transform your practice to attract more affluent patients.** In case you're wondering, there are a number of ways I might do this for you. For example, I might show you how to

...**reposition your practice** to distinguish your business from competitors who offer deep discounts.

...**target affluent patients** based on *'Affinity Marketing'* principles which help you easily form an emotional bond with prospects to build trust quickly. *(The affluent must trust you before they hire you.)*

...**pull in affluent patients** from untapped sources such as Facebook and Google PPC -- (*Your competition doesn't know how easy this can be when done the way I do it. This has nothing to do with SEO*).

And like I said, there's *no charge* for this.

Why Would I Make You Such An INSANE OFFER?

Two reasons: **First of all,** I enjoy it...

This type of thing is what I do best. It makes me very happy to see my expertise help a business transform into a medical practice with more affluent patients than they can handle.

Second of all, it's how I attract top-level clients to my inner-circle...

I love the science of selling without really selling. That's what I'm doing right now with you. It's how I want to transform your practice to help you attract more affluent patients.

Here's how it works...

Assuming you're happy and you want me to crank out these types of plans for you all the time...you'll probably want us to continue working together long term so I can help you with implementation.

You might be wondering what all of this is going to cost, right?

Well, it's not cheap, however...

If you think about it...**it really doesn't "cost" you anything**.

Let me explain...

I expect to **make you much more than $9,750 in the first month**...and if we keep working together over the next 12 months. I'm confident I can double your entire practice ...at minimum.

And look. If you don't want to become a client, don't worry about it. You won't get any sales pitch or pressure from me of any kind -- Ever.

Affluent patients are fun to work with.

They complain less.

They follow your recommendations.

They're not focused on fees, and you can charge them more for superior service.

They actually expect to pay you more!

Best of all, **they make your practice recession-proof in this "New Economy"**.

But, consider this...

THIS IS NOT FOR EVERYBODY AND, THIS MAY NOT BE RIGHT FOR YOU

I'm VERY picky about who I'll speak with and I've got a strict *(but reasonable)* set of criteria that needs to be met in order for us to proceed. Here it is:

1. **You have to have a solid medical practice already.**

    This offer is for medical professionals who are up and running already and simply want to run a lot faster and a lot farther. You should be doing around *$750k to seven figures or more each year* already...with a burning hunger for more.

2. **You must have a steady flow of leads and patients.**

    This means that you're getting consistent prospect flow and converting them into patients already. You're running ads, you're promoting, and you're hungry to test new media to attract new high networth patients.

    If you get 95% of your business from a referral network and you can't imagine spending money to test new media...you don't qualify. You don't have to be "everywhere" or "huge" ...I just need you to be PRESENT in your market.

3. **You must have a prospect-patient list.**

    It doesn't really need to be that big, just responsive. *(In this case: Size actually doesn't matter!)*

4. **You must have a good reputation, and superior service that patients brag about.**

   Everything we do together will not only bring you more affluent patients, but we'll be doing it in a way that creates MASSIVE goodwill in your market.

   In order for us to do that, you need to have your act together with no scandals, legal actions, or pending disputes in the air. *(We have enough of that infecting the political environment in Washington!)*

5. **You MUST follow directions. (Don't worry, I won't ask you to do anything weird or kinky.)**

   After all, if you don't actually implement the stuff I give you, neither one of us will make money.

That's it! Those are all my requirements.

HERE'S WHAT I WANT YOU TO DO NEXT

If you meet the criteria above and would like to talk about developing a blueprint to get you incredible results... then I'll happily set aside some time for you. However...

Due to the intense, one-on-one personalized nature of my consulting practice, I can only work with a handful of new clients. If you wait too long to contact me, I'll place you on my waiting list in case a spot opens in the future.

Here's how the process works...

First, you'll need to fill in out an application. Don't worry. It's simple and unobtrusive. I just need to know some details about your medical practice, and to get an idea of what you want to accomplish in the next 12-months.

Second, it takes me about 2 business days to review your application and decide if I can help you -- (and to determine whether or not your practice meets my qualifications)

HERE'S WHAT WILL HAPPEN AFTER THAT...

Pat or Stacy from my office will email you to set up a time for us to talk. We use email to set things up to avoid the dreaded "phone-tag" merry-go-round.

Pat and Stacy have been my right- and left-hands since 2010...and are my ONLY employees. One of them will contact you in about 48 business hours at the most.

Our initial call will be between 30 and 45 minutes.

This is where we really begin figuring out exactly what you want ...and how to make it happen.

I'll painstakingly review your goals, positioning with prospects, and so forth ...and I'll deliver a plan to bring in more affluent patients for you.

If you see value in becoming a high level client, great!

We can talk about it.

If you don't want to become a client - that's OK too. No biggie.

WARNING - TIME IS A FACTOR

This opportunity is extremely limited because of the intense one-on-one time needed to provide you with results. Therefore, it's physically impossible for me to work with more than a handful of people.

Once I reach my capacity, I will accept no more clients...period.

I enjoy my free time outside the office.

Also, you should realize there's a very large demand for personal one-on-one help from me -- *and what I'm offering to you is unprecedented* -- and a bit insane.

So with that said, know that the window of opportunity won't be open long.

If you feel like this is right for you, go to http://chrissewelldigitalmedia.nyc/discovery/ and fill out the application and let's talk.

Talk soon,

Chris Sewell

www.ingramcontent.com/pod-product-compliance
Lightning Source LLC
Chambersburg PA
CBHW071645170526
45166CB00003B/1437

* 9 7 8 1 5 1 9 2 8 5 0 8 9 *